E Braveheart has a twin sister and an older brother. She had an older sister who sadly passed away a couple of years ago. She was born into a working-class family. Due to physical health problems and home life, she missed a lot of school, so left with no qualifications. However, she has a wealth of knowledge from the school of life. She has major mental health issues which affect every part of her life.

My greatest thanks to Dr Reeves, a truly remarkable family GP. For over eleven years, you listened and talked to me. I've lost count of how many times you have saved my life.

To Dr Turri, thank you for spending so long listening and explaining things to me.

Thank you to my twin sister for standing by me and thank you to my wonderful new stepdad.

E Braveheart

THE CHILD SOLDIERS

AUSTIN MACAULEY PUBLISHERS™

LONDON • CAMBRIDGE • NEW YORK • SHARJAH

A CIP catalogue record for this title is available from the British Library.

ISBN 9781035804436 (Paperback)
ISBN 9781035804443 (ePub e-book)
ISBN 9781035817788 (Audiobook)

www.austinmacauley.com

First Published 2023
Austin Macauley Publishers Ltd®
1 Canada Square
Canary Wharf
London
E14 5AA

Thank you to Austin Macauley Publishers for giving me this chance to fulfil a 40-year dream of mine.

Foreword

I hope you enjoy reading these poems. Some are light hearted, others a little heavier going. Maybe you'll find some common ground in some. If, for any reason, you are reading one which is on the darker side and realise that you are thinking or feeling similar things, please talk to someone, it really does help. You are not alone.

There are so many different types of Mental Illnesses caused by so many different things. Like thousands of other people, mine was caused by early childhood trauma. That child dictates how I think, feel, see the world and interact with it.

The children are the only truly innocent ones of this world. It is the job of all of us to protect them at all costs.

I know life can sometimes get in the way. Whatever your dream is, keep going for it. Please don't listen to fools who tell you, "It's rubbish, it will never happen, blah, blah, blah." Keep going for it, keep fighting for it. One day it will come true.

Thank you.

It Doesn't Help

When you're gay it doesn't help
To see people disintegrate your hope for today
Sniggers behind your overweighed arched back
Curse at your soul
It doesn't help to be black
Dreams give you strength that you need to be free
Walking alone unknown through billowing trees of coldness
and unkindness
It doesn't help to be loveless
When tangles of overground weeds tackle your heart of no
cruelness
A need of staggering pain
You're crying out through your pouring vain
Your unloved soul forever does scream
It doesn't help to be different
The messages from heaven that are to you sent
Believing in freedom and justice
People's understanding of you always seem to miss
Murdered by another humans influence
You too murder another
A scared conscience lives within a drifter
It doesn't help to murder
Drinking heavily because of fear

Dropping more days off your fading years
You're human but no one cares
No more human
Your soul of love, to love it no longer can
Because of the things that have happened
Hatred tries to weave its way in
Sex. It's not for me
It doesn't help
To feel sick at the thought of the human bodies that are
continually bought
No marriage, no children
Your hopeless love for no one
It doesn't help
Unbelieving unkindness hatred there is no less
No wonder a sulk is sussed
No friends no enemies
To other suffering countries over the screaming sea
To meet another me
But
It doesn't help you see.

The Wedding Day

Our hearts go out for Lady Di and Charles
On their wedding day
We'll all cheer and feel pride as he slips the ring of love onto
her finger
The whole nation will feel joy and happiness,
As they walk to their carriage full in blossom
As flowers first opening in spring
Their perfume of love for one another,
Will be smelt from all parts of the world Lady Di and
Charles, forever be happy
And in love for one another.

Here No More

My life seems so unreal
My sadness too sad to be true
Days fade into nights of dreams
Never to come true
But still the hope lives within me
For reasons I do not know
So depressed my soul
My mind so empty but still so whole
The memories that drive me
I live to remember
The face I long to see lives within me
I know I should be grateful
For such happy memories
But how can I be happy
She's no longer with me.

Grey Squirrel

Grey squirrel, grey squirrel
Come sit by my side
So sleek and shy
Your independence beauty
Are beauty to any eyes
So warming through to the heart
Your independence and beauty that make you so different
from any other animal
From land, sea, or sky
So light on your feet, you scurry from treetop to treetop
You scurry from harsh men who chop down your homes
Grey squirrel
Grey squirrel
Come sit by my side
So sleek and shy.

The Mood

The mood
I've got to be in the mood
If the mood tis not right
The move is also not right
For I need the feelings to write how I feel
I need the atmosphere to be just right
Maybe I live by my moods
So different to my every move
Without them how could I be
So different from you?
So distant is how I like to be,
To write,
To indulge in my words of crime and violence
Of love and friendships
Of understanding, not hating.
For I need the mood to be just right
For my certain move of the night.

Red Squirrel

Red squirrel, red squirrel
Asleep on my lap
Do you feel comfort there you don't feel elsewhere?
Your rarity and beauty do make you as one
You're one of the animals that I adore
Your brother, grey squirrel, as light on his feet as you are,
Scurrying from treetop to treetop,
Scurrying from harsh men who chop down your homes,
Red squirrel
Red squirrel
Do you feel comfort there you don't feel elsewhere.

The Mist

The mist
The dark mist descends
Engulfing, wrapping my entity,
Engulfing my body and spirit,
Blocking out the sun, dispersing any hope.
Draining my strength, my spirit.
Trying, trying to run,
You can't escape the mist.
It descends, engulfing me, blocking out any hope.
The only thing left is eternal peace
May God take me into his arms.
Take me to pastures of green fields,
Of trees gently swaying, of picnics filled with laughter.
The suffocating mist, choking me.
Draining the life out of me.
Draining any hope.
Give me peace, please give me peace.
No more pain.
Peace, peace, peace.

The English Rose

The English Rose, she sits nestled in the borders.
Mixed with the tall flowers that shadow her beauty.
She watches you with empathy.
Her colours swathe in sunlight to give you encouragement to go on.
Her delicate perfumed petals tell you she hears your pain, she wants to listen.
Take a look, a closer look.
She fights the elements that surround her.
Touch her lightly, give her the inspiration to go on.
She fights the wind, the rain, the drought.
Water her gently, shelter her from the harshest of winds.
Give her the encouragement to keep growing.
To keep her beautiful petals flowering.
Her colours so bright, help her fight to survive,
Talk to her gently, her wisdom shines through.
Her colours of integrity are there for you.
Louise, the English Rose.

The Child Soldiers

The war that go on behind closed doors
The children's cries that go unheard
The bruises and broken bones hidden by excuses
They sit shaking while their parents guzzle beer and shout
and fight
They break up the violence using their bodies as bollards
They clean up the vomit and look after their alcoholic
mothers
They clean and stop the dads from killing their mothers
Warzones leave scars that the unseeing cannot see
Don't forget these children, they are the future for you and
me
Theirs scares leaving them an outcast from communities
Acknowledge their heroism
They gave themselves to protect their families
They deserve medals too
A medal of peace to block the flashbacks and anxieties
The mental scars that no one sees
Praise these children, open your eyes
What's happening next door, do these soldiers live next door
to you?
The sexual abuse a secret shame, the mental torture and
emotional damage handed out like candy

The child soldier lives on in adult bodies
Give these children a medal for the peace they deserve.

By My Whiskers

Pussy cat, pussy cat, how did you get here?
I saunter through the garden,
By my whisker's I steer.
The mice and birds know to stay well clear.
I stealthily approach *as* quiet as can be.
My whiskers, my compass,
They tell me the spaces through which I can squeeze.
By touch, by the winds breeze,
I can find my way to my prey.
If you're lucky enough to be in your lap I will lie.
Just don't mess with my whiskers,
They're as sensitive as your ears.
Stroke me gently and I will purr, warming your lap.
Gently, gently this pussy cat is here.
Treat me kindly and your companion I'll be.
Forever great friends and allies we'll be.

I Wonder Where I'll Go

See ya, up or down
I wonder where I'll go
Only fools really know
My heart is true
It's passionate love holds no falling snow
Dreams of long ago,
In my departing soul do still grow
Through the coming years my justice for freedom will not
fear
Oh yeah, oh yeah
To you, I'll sing in an enriched melody
Hold back your hatred
Bring forth your understanding
Like an old crackling playing record that is scratched
Still as clear as spring water comes the loving
Through the fantasies comes the song
See ya
Up or down, I wonder where I'll go
Only God really knows
To be condemned or to be freed
Only the Lord Christ sees
The dreams of reality that hold no disappointing greed

For years it seems for the unwilling understanding, not
hating
For you I live, all my life to give.

Forgiveness

Forgiveness comes from within, it helps you unload,
the lightness back in.
It carries its own energy, letting it ground you.
Mother and father who greatly sinned against you,
Forgive them their faults they had, they suffered from their
grievances too.
So caught up in their pain, they couldn't see what they were
doing to you.
Leaving you with deep scars, the pain, the pain that you
cannot see.
Another generation cut with the onslaught of patterns that do
harm yet again.
The cycle keeps turning, generation to generation.
Forgive them, forgive them.
Try not to do the same as they so often did
God or no God,
Let the forgiveness wash from your shoulders the years of
blame.
Lift you out of the burden of pain.
Forgive them, forgive them.
Halt the cycle of pain and blame.
Forgive them.

The Tattoo Parlour

Come into my parlour,
I'll give you the pleasure of the pain, you so much desire.
It's only a scratch here and there after all.
You'll want to be back for more.
Give me your design, and I'll give you what your heart
desires.
You'll keep coming back for more.
Give me the design, and I'll stay with you forever.
Scratching, scratching, a little more ink and colour here.
You'll be back for more. I'll get under your skin.
See you next time, though you'll say no more not again.
Take care of me, and I'll do you proud.
A walking canvas, we'll share our art with the world aloud.

Thoughts of a Dying Man

As I lay here with my eyelids growing heavier, I wonder will
I wake up to the new light of day
Will my dreams just fade away, when asleep
Memories drift through my decaying mind
Thoughts of loved ones lost
But I know, I'm to die unknown
Put me in my unknown grave of darkness
It's all I'm paid for my crying out in pain, of these long
fading days
What have I done to deserve this cancer eating my brain
away
Always done as much good as I could
For I know, I may never see the new light of day
Nor hear the birds singing gayly to start the new day.

The Merry Go Round

I want to get off the merry-go-round, the merry-go-round,
the merry-go-round, the merry-go-round
I want to get off the merry-go-round, the merry-go-round,
the merry-go-round, the merry-go-round.
I want this life to end, the sadness washed away.
You say I'm this, you say I'm that, none of it's a fact.
Don't call me paranoid just because
I see and hear things you don't recognise.
Stop this ride, I want to get off.
Give me the peace so I can hide.
Surrounded by glass, the world
I cannot touch it.
I hear the sweet music, the laughter, and the happiness,
But I'm not invited, I don't belong.
The world sees me as an easy thing to break.
The monster I carry inside is taunting me.
The people see it, and run and hide.
This ride has gone wrong, let me off.
I want to die for the peace it will bring.
In this unforgiving world, there's no place to hide.
You say I'm being manipulative when I'm only trying to be
nice.

You say I'm making threats, when the truth in me does not hide.

Here we go on the merry go round, up and down, up and down.

I want to get off, I've had enough, let me have the peace I need.

Trying to keep living but the world keeps throwing ammo.

Is it a life worth living?

This existence so painful, a life not worth living.

Is it worth saving...............? NO?

The Lone Wolf

The lone wolf howls longingly into the night.
How did she become so separated from her pack?
She searches into ever widening circles, frantic, crying.
You won't see her, she sleeks back into the shadows.
Searching, more desperate for the comfort of her fellows.
She cries alone, searching for any scent that may show her
the way back to her pack.
She's a warrior, but alone she's not meant to be.
She's a survivor, but the others make her complete.
Howling louder, more confused and lost.
Howling longer, she's in desperate need of her kin.
A beautiful creature of the night, she's tired now, alone she
cannot survive.
She needs her companions to feed.
Howls long and pitiful, she sends shivers down your spine
She carries on searching,
A howling soulful wolf, the lone wolf.

The Devil's Pit

Ahhhhh, clinging on by my fingertips
Don't let me fall into this pit.
Pull me up, please oh God pull me up!
The darkness is calling my name.
Don't let me drown.
I want to breathe, to feel the sunlight on my face.
Oh God help me, the devil is up to his tricks again.
Pull, pull me hard with all your strength.
I'm struggling to breathe.
He's calling out my name, the devil with so many faces.
Curse him down, don't let me fall
Let the summer breeze re-freshen my soul from shame.
Pull me up, I want to smile again.

The Words I Could Not Speak

I thought he was loving me
The words I could not speak.
What a torment
The torment, the torment.
For years it followed me,
My years engulfed in torment,
For years and years.
Let it go.
Let it unwrap from your heart.
Let it go, let it go.
Let the light in,
Let the burden lift.
It wasn't your fault,
Just a child you'd be.
Let her grow, flourish into a springtime for you.
Let the burden be gone,
Into a free woman, into the sunshine walk free.

The Shame

The shame, the shame.
The shame of being lonely,
Don't admit to it.
The shame of being lonely does cast its shadow, does
destroy the soul's gift of life.
The loneliness, loneliness… not being able to interact with
the world.
The people's stares, the judgement they cast.
Why don't you fit, why *don't* you belong?
The loneliness belittles me, erodes me, despises myself for
giving myself to the world.
The loneliness that kills will be the end of me.
It will kill your fondest of your memories of me.
Kill your tears, kill your love.
The loneliness filled with such shame has no regret of the
sadness it brings.
The shame, the shame that loneliness brings.
I bow to your weight, I bow to your burden.
I cry into the night.
Of the energy of impacting to the human world
I cannot touch.
This loneliness will finally kill me, forget me not.

This Anger

This anger, this anger
Where will it go?
This anger that simmers and bubbles, this anger that boils
and quakes.
The child within which no one would hear, shouts out in
anger
"Will anyone listen to my cries, my sorrow to hear"
The abused one crouched over in pain and fear.
Listen to her anger, frustration and tears.
This anger, this anger that boils and quakes, threatens all
boundaries that humankind make.
This anger, this anger that threatens all sanity.
Give it a voice, so it no longer holds strength.
This anger, this anger, give it a voice that someone will hear.
To start the healing process, to throw away the pain and fear.
For peace to set in a child so small.
To give her a chance at happiness forever if bold.
A chance at life once again.

In the Darkness

Are you coming?

Are you coming with love?

Sketches, notes, and my little black book with little black words, pictures of now, of the future, of the past, of blood.

I'm not mad. It's only a part of me that's given in, that's come loose.

What good did it do, talking to that psychologist?

It's in the wardrobe at home, the notebook, here there are only crumbs, apples and everything that needs doing, that's already done and needs doing again.

Let me in, do you hear?

It's cold out here. Let me in.

Why are you laughing?

Your laughter is tearing me apart.

It's cold and damp, I want to go home.

But this is probably my home now.

I want to join in and play.

Receive some love.

That's all.

I Fought the War

I fought the war
Now I'm losing the battle
Day by day, my life ebbs away
Constantly reliving the memories
Trapped in a hell created by a sick love
I gave so much for others
Now only shown coldness, there is no love
Validate my presence, everything I gave
Please God help me, I can't live with this pain
Wipe the slate clean as I have done for others.

Man, Oh Man

You've saved my life so many times.
You've listened to my pain.
You've held me close when I thought I was dead.
You've been the man, oh man.
Though the tears run silently down my face,
You place your hand on my knee,
And again, I'm part of the human race.
Man, oh man, you're the man.
You speak softly from the heart, from experience of your own.
Your soft eyes touch me.
Your voice calms my pain
Man, oh man, you're the man.
In the dark pit of sorrow, you pull me up into the light,
The sun is warming my skin.
Sending the sorrow to the dark woods.
You've stood next to me, my next of kin.
Man, oh man, you're the man.

Thou Flowers Thee

Though thou flowers may crumple and wither away,
Onto the ground where thee one day shall be laid in my final
resting days
Throughout the evading years
Thou that pass too quickly to become the good old yesteryear
My heart may be saddened to hear the unsettled farewells
Choking my songs of praise
Strangling my crystallised tears of the precious memories
Sunshine comes gleaming through the overcasting shadowing
clouds
Warming sun rays, the perfection of the hawthorns hopeful
eye
Oh, world of ingratitude thrash your injustice on thee no more
Tender the gardens with rainbows, with life
Of thee sweet asylum, honeysuckle and strawberries
The subtle stems of caressing beauty
Thou petals of comforting sweetness
Thy art thou servant to watch over thee
While cold nights wonder
To keep our bustling bees singing while they hum to thyme
and coriander
Forever I will tender thee
In the final resting place

I will love thee
Oh, flowers of joy of sadness of peace
Thou perfect blossoms that comfort thee.

First Love

For the first time in my life
Someone wants me, thinks I'm nice
Though I can't help thinking, something's bound to go wrong
Boredom sets in, becomes an unrealistic dream
Does she love me, can I love her?
Fingers touch, bodies twist and glisten
You're the first to hold me
The first I've let to undress me
Days and nights we groan together, passing slowly the time
comes for me to phone, are you in
Or has our new love gone cold
A hello, how are you
Seconds pass, I want to know you
The devil sits in his wicked chair
Watch his smirk as he commands you his dares
Keep a watchful eye out for temptations are never far away
Say yes to a dance, you have a clear conscience
Say no to the bed cover, you love another
You're the first to want me
So, let's be kind, our honesty can reward lost time
Take away our masks, throw them to the ravages of crime
Be mine tonight, forever we may last.

Pleasant Sounds

People laughing with joy
People laughing with happiness
Morning birds singing with happiness
These pleasant sounds come to my ears
To make me feel better, not for worse
The not quite silent messages from the unseen God
Into our souls are given
The wind blows through the gentle swaying tree tops
That we little hear and little see
Rainwater glides down the sloping cliff
Making a river for all the fish
The soft crispin' noise under my feet, made from the icicles
Of dew of the early morning spring.

Love Is a Funny Thing

Love, it's a funny thing
It makes you cry at silly songs
It makes you so strong but it makes you so weak
Remembering yesterday you smile
It makes you live in despair at the thought of a no tomorrow
You don't want to keep on living
But you can't kill yourself
Because you know you've got to keep on living in hope
That love will come back someday tomorrow
You die in tomorrow
Living for another maybe today
Remembering the only love you had yesterday
It's an actor at disguising you
You sit on a pedal stool
Making you laugh at her show
It's really making you cry inside
And that's not a happy low
When I see a star looking up, and there you are
Baby I love you
Happiness, it's never been true
Love, it's a funny thing
One romantic candle lit dinner
And a whole meaningful life you can gain

In a single argument you can lose it all again
Love makes you mean
It makes your soul go mouldy green
Love, it makes you give your heart, with a cuddly grin
Love, it's a funny thing.

Romeo, Romeo

Romeo, Romeo. Where art thou Romeo

Soppy, soppy yuck

I will not love

No love, no sex

No man will intertwine himself in my human body's soul

My gayness will forever grow

Throughout the ages

Through time and you

Through up amongst the stars

I'll smile through the heavens onto you

For God loves us all, however large or small

Through the crisp air we hear his call

All for love and understanding

Fasten your seatbelts for the landing

Back down to earth from our dreams

We've arrived back home

The earth like an overgrown melon

Cripples it's lovers with a crippling rebellion

Aids the sickness we fear

Gays are kicked down through the other persons fear Romeo,

Romeo where art thou Romeo

Soppy, soppy yuck

I will not love

No love
No sex
No man will intertwine himself in my bodily soul
My gayness will forever grow.

Forget It Chums

Forget it chums
Never alone, never a bum
Always working all year through
I dream of you, ideals of loving, loving only me
Working for a low sum
Never searching
All year round I wait for you
I fantasise of writing
Becoming a legend in my own lifetime
Looking ahead will it come
No brains locked with time in chains
Somewhere it will come through clear
In a world of disasters
When I am nightly in the years of fear
The world still trembles, fearing nuclear war
My body aches with squashing sores
When will I love with a passionate cure?
Forget it chums
Never alone, never a bum
Always working all year through
Hearts echo with creasing yells of pain
But nothing stays the same
Pasting past stays here, never moving

It's never clear
Drunks drink beer, alcoholics anonymous
Crashing buses
Glowing red lights of prostitutes of homersexuals
Their love is right
I am gay so what
I never will be free
I never will be understood, I am a homersexual
I'm a bum,
Forget it chums.

To Me This Is Nothing

Only time can decide who's to live and who's to die
My body hunts for life
Out of my body I scan myself
Horror movies of my past are in my dreams
Tears scream through my body's memories so vast
Violence creating fear
My forgiveness pleads
To forgive all the hatred throughout the years
To me this is nothing
But what if life is a spinning wheel of fantasy
No good for today
It's only building tears
Nothing that exists can bring me harm
Selfishness to bring hope of finding love
She sleeps within my nightmares
The golden age of all that's true
Nothing is all this
It's just a painting, a brush of life
Magic water trickles down our faces of nothing
With all these things I think
All the emotions I humbly drink
I'm drunk with a repulsive round of life
All false of truths

Friends and family
Persons questions of things so personal
Of gays and prostitutes
It's a job not politeness
Nothing is all this.

Our Silent Charlie Chaplin

Our silent Charlie Chaplin
So silent, his lips curve with a soundless magic
His funny optimistic grin
Opens up a mountain from within
A fountain of laughter we all sort after
Wobbling from side to side
With his walking stick by his side
Like a rabbit he twitches his nose
Through the deepening snow through the streets
His acting forever giving us a lasting treat
Silent Charlie Chaplin
Through the sky above comes the glistening sun
So too do you your laughter comes
But did you nether explore a private life
Laughing Charlie did you ever cry
Through the openings of the sky
Do you blush or are you never shy
Wearing a black bowler hat and black baggy trousers
Have you ever sat on a lovers' mat
Did you never explore the land of losers?
Our silent Charlie Chaplin
A laughing legend of kindness
A sad character in your silent movies

With no loving next of kin
But you always win with a laughing grin
Our silent Charlie Chaplin is still working on
Through the heavens
Our silent Charlie Chaplin.

A War

A war places discomfort in the minds of good men
Weapons of destruction from factories painted with blood
These foolish things we send
Without signs of embarrassment president's wipe out the uncontrolled countries
Countries helplessly surrender
But not without us hearing their cries
Peace clings without the glue of love,
To the heartbroken minds of unbroken men
Horror besieges the clean gloves of the unmarked child
Men turn dangerously wild killing ragged clothed men
Who no longer wear the soldier's uniform
No antiseptic for the wounded
Through their decaying bodies limbs are sworn,
With a blade of blood of no free man
A curse of evil a down payment on foolish men
Who are no longer civil?
Fighting with a wrecking vengeance
We come to the end of our world
No longer do we see our world with a hope
Or glimpse of common sense
To the end with a war.

No More Hate Can I Find

No More hate can I find, no longer can I unwind
From the pressures and views of the unsightly few
I can no longer find the hate from the world
That separates, I hate not you
For understanding is my view
Understand and you will not find hate
Hate, and hatred you will create
I hate no one
For if I hate I will be hated
What good does hatred do
Is it as sweet as a lovers kiss?
Does it meet with sure bliss with friendship?
Friends help more you can be sure than hatred
Hatred makes me cry
Understanding keeps me living one more day
No happiness comes from hating
But only loneliness
Understand don't hate
The only way to feel great.

The Lonely Winter Filled Garden

Feelings
Left with a heartbreak of memories
Falling in love time after time
But left alone at the end of the road of time
I often wonder if it's worthwhile
Falling in love with a no tomorrow
My heart begins to harden in the lonely winter filled garden,
To a sadness we're all dreading
Emotions grasp at an invisible love that leave a mark we see
That blindly decorate you and me
To find a brilliant shining love in the sky of this garden
My gasping heart lives only with reinforcing hope
Searching for a love, I find my waiting lover
My yesterday's past cleanly wiped away
To be forgotten
My soul warmly alights
I find a love that will always have sight
Through the rusting doors of time, we pass into a new tomorrow
Filled with a love that will grow
A friendship of no more sorrow
Because we have a tomorrow.

Pusey Cat, Pusey Cat

Pusey cat, pusey cat
Little and so very sweet
Looking through your eyes, both our hearts meet
A love for you, and a love for me
A playful joy shining playful memories
That we play in harmony
So smooth and subtle
Your fur glides along your back
Your inquisitive eyes
Your humming ears
Make me feel you'll always be here
Pounce on my toes
It just goes to show your kitten's joy
You nether feel low.

Never Goodbye

Never goodbye, somehow
There's been no change in my mind
I still love you, but is that kind
Do you want to live your own life?
And never want to see me again
Oh, how I'd cry
If you were to say goodbye
I dream of how it might have been
Your love warming my soul
And making it glow
I'll never say goodbye to my memories of you
They'll always be a part of me
If I knew where you live
To you I'd give all the love that makes me live
Here am I waiting for you
My tears, my memories forever killing me
I'll never say goodbye till the day I die.

A Room of Time

A room
The walls are white
A framed picture of a bride and groom hangs on a wall
Shining in the morning sunlight
An open window brings into today's charm
In a breeze that will disperse tomorrow
A butterfly flutters with calm
Into the settling dust of time
But emotions escape into the atmosphere
Leaving the fading photographs to unwind
Forgetting fear, silent laughter
Hushed lovers leave their memories in past summers
Memories, feelings
Revolving into an atmosphere of time
Keeping love within a room of time.

I Love Someone

I love someone
I will not say who because I don't want you
To hurt the person, I love
I love her with all my heart, soul and mind
And oh, how I wish she could be mine
But she's gone far away, over the sea
And can't you see how much she means to me
I dream of her returning
And this is all that keeps me living
I live in a daze
In memories of yesterday
And maybe today I'll see her
All will be as yesterday
But as yet this is far away
But still I'll be here hoping another day
Like a cloak over my heart I wear
To keep in the love that is already there
And because of great warmth I hold for her
The love keeps growing
And never will disappear.

Reading My Home Town

Reading my home town
I've lived here for so long
Never am I gone for long without returning,
To the ever changing town
Old and new interlock contrasting, mixing there's such a lot
Busy streets, bustling with window shoppers
Sundays lonesome until the pubs close
Screams echo through the deserted streets
But who's around to know
But still I'm here watching the scenery change
The old will go
But still some will remain
The noise and dirt forms a picture frame
Containing a changing picture of time
And it won't be long before I'm no longer around
But I'm still hanging on to my memories of the past
I don't want to die, and my past can't say goodbye
So I'll live to remember and to hope
That time will restart.

Trapped in Yesterday

Always dreaming but what good does it do me?
Never a single inch further down the road
Always hoping in dreams that can only form false hopes
But still these dreams over take my mind
My heart is over-spilling of dreams that time can never find
I have few thoughts of the real world about me
My only world
Are dreams found inside of me
But still I dream
For the pleasures they bring
That is when I'm dreaming these things
My only world are the dreams formed in me
But still I dream
For the pleasures they bring
That is when I'm dreaming these things
But when I stop, the sorrow overtakes the pleasure of dreaming
I cry for a person
Who the world cannot allow me to love me
I'll always wait for this person
For my dreams are my prison of feelings of time
I'll always cry for her, because I'll always love her

My dreams are my hope
That she'll love me.

Please Miss Don't Go

Please miss, don't go, I need you
No one told me of your leaving, only my dreams of the night
I couldn't stand a single day, knowing you weren't there no more
Oh, miss please don't go
Don't leave me all alone in this big horrible world
I need you
I need your loving smiles and the laughter
They're the only pleasures the world holds for me
Please don't go
When I haven't heard the three words my heart wants to hear the most
The three words my heart holds out for you
Please don't leave them, take them
Don't break my young heart, I love you
Take them now
Please miss before you go
Without you hearing them I'll have no more need to live
You're the only person my heart has room for.

You

You never take any notice of me
You're always away in the arms of the man that hit you
You say he's changed
I can't seem to believe that
When we left him so
I know we thought we would be happy for once
But still we're not
I still live in fear for the safety of you, my mother
You're hurting me once more
You don't seem to know how it also hurt me so
When we went into our new lives of more agony and pain
Why can't you see I can't go back to see him hit you more?
I don't want to go back
Because I love you so
My thoughts of you going back, are eating my life and brain
away
You've changed me,
You don't seem to love me anymore.

To Miss

The first day I saw her, she rebuilt my life
But feelings came through I never thought I had
For love and care came her way, though she never knew
Those three years were the best years of my life,
Though my home life was so incomplete
Oh I love her
The memories echo on
Feelings, oh feelings
Feelings showing through I never knew
Please Miss you nether knew how you restored my life
My life so incomplete until you
Please Miss, please Miss, don't just walk away
I have this urge to tell you of these things
I know so truly so many people
I can't turn to because they're not you
Oh, please miss listen to the truth
Oh, oh, please I love you, that's the truth
Please don't go away, I wouldn't be the same without you
Again my life would be so dull and incomplete without you.

Lover's Worry

When nothing seems to be going right, don't worry
I'll be here holding your hand all night
Just rest your worrying head on my shoulder
Problems will always be coming our way
But together we'll pass through to the new light of day
Oh, darling we'll be together
Love holding our heads on each other's shoulder of care
Nothing will part us, we'll always be as one
From early morning to sunset we'll be holding hands
All the work and pleasures of life to be done
Will be done with love and care
Don't worry, don't worry, I'll be here
We'll dream, our lover's dreams all through the night
And in the morning we'll be as one
Going through our problems, not with hate for life
But with love and care,
Holding us together, through to the new light of day.

The Fountain

The flowing fountain of knowledge
The stream of kindness, flows cascading through you
You listen gently explaining what's happening
You tell me off gently when I'm in the wrong
To look after your family, you are doing your best
How can that be wrong?
You show you're a human, a worthwhile case
You work so hard to show you care
You go above what you should do, so tired are you
Please don't desert me, I hear myself cry
But to better your future you must follow your path
You care so much what happens to us
You fight for my corner when everyone else says no
We don't want you to do that, for you to go
But the future of you and your family must come first, this we
know
I wish you the best because you have given your all
You're one of the good guys, I'll miss you so much
Boundaries unknown of what to do and say
When the thought of you going makes me cry
I shouldn't be a shellfish
You've tried and you've tried

I wish you much happiness, your future bright, free from the
nightmare of living day by day
You've been so gentle, your knowledge unbound, you've kept
me alive in the darkest of times
All I can say is thank you
Please don't leave me in the desert, the vultures are circling,
they're out to get me, to put me in the ground
Thank you for caring, your kindness unbound
Thank you for your support when everyone else put me down.

A Helping Hand

Through my tears you patiently listened
You heard the pain creep out from within my tears
You asked the Questions and heard me
While others often asked, they couldn't hear my pain
The avalanche of shame that came crashing down around my ears
They gave up on me without seeing the small child that remains inside me
Locked up deep within the fear
You heard the scars that shout up louder than my tears
You offered me a helping hand
Another way of dealing with the anguish
You offered me hope instead of constant despair
To be human again, a life to regain
You didn't have to be here
To do what you have done
You offered me warmth and kindness, when I believed it had all gone
You heard the child within me
You've given me different tools to work with
To be part of the human train again
While others have judged me harshly, you saw that I can be kind

All I can say is thank you and try to do my best
I hope that this repays you
I'll be forever in your debt
Thank you.

He's the One

I'm so depressed deep inside
Because of the things going on around me
No one knows how I feel
Because no one asks how I feel
She keeps saying she's going back
She says, "Because he's changed"
And won't beat her black
I don't want to go back
She doesn't know how it hurt me so
To see her get kicked in the head
I don't want to go back
These frightening memories keep coming back.
I can't go back
Because of these things, running around in my head
She doesn't take notice of the things that I do
She's only concerned of the man who beat her black and blue
He's the one who destroyed her.

Be My Friend

I thought you were my friend
The only one in the world.
But even you,
You've turned against me
Because of the good I was trying to do.
Now I'm alone
When you're alone, I'll be your friend.
Even when you're not mine
Make up your mind
What must I do to become your friend?
I don't ask much of anyone
I only ask not to be on my own.
When you've got everything, you can have
You don't notice what others don't have.
I am not a rich person,
I don't ask for fame
I only ask for a friend.
That means a lot, to one with no friends.

The Sun Is Shining in My Heart

The sun is shining in my heart
The birds are singing too.
When I see you,
You put joy in my heart.
I didn't use to know what love really meant.
But since I met you it's been here in my heart.
The sun has been shining in my life since I met you.
I haven't touched the ground,
Since I first saw you.
You brought something new into my life.
You made me realise what lies in life,
For me and you.
I love you.
The words echo through my heart.
Now the sun is shining in my heart for you.

Loving

Loving is a painful thing
A thing of heartbreak and sorrow
I've had little love,
But because of it, there is much sadness in my heart.
Your heart breaks in two,
When love is no more.
Why is it no more?
That was once in both hearts.
It destroys your mind.
Your peace of living is no more.
To love when you've had no love,
Is a hard thing to consider.
To try to love,
As you would have liked to have been loved.
You give all you can,
But none is returned in your hand,
To the centre of your heart.

A Craggy Shoreline

Pebbles, pebbles, under my feet
So hard, so bumpy, like crocodile's feet.
The seas creeping up at me,
I can feel it under my feet.
For nothing stands still forever,
Not the sea,
Not time, not me.
It's so cold out here in the morning breeze
The seas are busy with living things.
Even the shoreline with its greasy stones,
And uneven lines of seaweed.
So slimy and different in colour and size,
The smell gets right up your nose.
So different from lead,
So exposed in our streets and homes.
Seagulls gliding so high in the sky.
Their wings stretching,
Their cries are crying.
They're not like you or me,
They are free.

Looking in the Mirror

Looking in the mirror, is that really me?
Surely it must be my enemy
It scares me
My soul can't describe why I feel the things I do
Why is it encased in a cruel untruthful you?
The beautiful things I feel are surrounded by an evil clinging glue
It doesn't look like me
Don't want to look into a mirror, is that really me?
Surely it must be my enemy
All I see is an untrue stranger
Looking in a mirror, eyes looking back at me
Like a cruel dishonest disease
Dark curly hair, teeth like daggers of strife
God, how can that be true?
God, you know how it scares me?
My soul can't believe with all the beautiful things it can build
It's mistaken for a thing like that
Please, oh God, don't bring it back
I've got a taste of blood in my mouth
It's that thing in there, in the mirror
It's making me mad
It's cutting my throat, ah

It's turning me mad, it's making me mad
Looking in the mirror, looking in the mirror
Ahhh!

Alone I Stand

Alone I stand in my darkened room, watching you
With evils of the past and the shadows that bind me
My souls surrounded by bars
My nightmares still silencing me
So alone I stand, watching you
The whole truth I cannot declare
For you my friends, I do not want to scare
Through the distant lanes of time
In the house so bleak, so black
I am cursed to remember a monster so cruel
Who stole my mind, who made me crack
So, alone I stand watching you
My conscience is my nightmare
That squeals and screams for peace
They steal my laughter.
No smiles can appear to grin upon my face
Oh people who never question my crime
Who accepted my faults are my friends so kind
Still alone I stand watching you
Time has passed and I've done my time
My nightmares are my conscience, my reminder
Of a monster too evil, so cruel
Of the pain I brought on you

I've made a mistake, I led my own downfall
To you all my friends, I showed you who the fool was
Still alone, I stand watching you
Reach out for me, to hold me tight
Bring me back to the soft sunlight
Wave away this worry
My friends, I'm so sorry
Set me free, forgive me.

What Am I Doing in a Place Like This

What am I doing in a place like this?
I have to ask myself
These people only human
Still they're so far away
Their minds incapable of controlling their own lives
People trying to help them
Scarcely knowing the unreachable truths behind their illness
Looking around, the locked doors the opaque one-way windows
Cardboard table and chairs
Make this a fairy-tale world
Filled with days that can only come out of a horror movie
The screaming zombies that the drugs do make
And who still don't help
A hand to embrace to conquer the fear
Could I'm sure do so much more
But still I'm in a place like this
The blocked-out views from which surround my new unholy fear
The punishment that seems so unfair
When just to be parted from our friends and homes
Is quite enough to bear

Cigarettes but once an hour
Meals on wheels through hatches
Like animals stubborn faces that no longer smile
A payment for a crime committed
A crime of such degree that I can no longer have my freedom
No night to commit suicide
Only the life of the sentenced
A dull and unhappy world intense with boredom
A place to sit and think of innocence
What am I doing in a place like this.

In This Disaster You Call a Cell

The walls that do creep forever closer
Moving on me, besieging me
The floor so cold pressing my heels so real
The ceiling so heavy that it falls down upon my head
Pressing into my mind, squashing out any thought of time
Oh this room I dread
Square opaque windows dressed in concrete
Drawing in closer to me moving in on my mind
Killing my mind
Deceiving everything
Oh, God please let me out
Won't you let an angel open the green door?
Where I press my forehead against the grate
Reminding me of green grass
That I can no longer choose to touch or smell
Oh, the thought in mind
In my throat these things bring a swell
You can choose to close your eyes to try to forget
Only to open them into a living nightmare
Screaming bodies in a torture chamber
No laughter
No happiness in this decreasing circle
This room that grows forever smaller

Moving in on me, engulfing my body
Pressing in on my exploding memories
That are too great to remember
But still not too small to be able to forget
The touching of loved ones
The remembrance of smell
In this disaster you call a cell.

Claire Rayner

When you read our letters, your eyes become your ears

You patiently welcome with an open heart, our searching questions

You're the goddess of the agony aunts

You're a reason for loving, for carrying on

Your sweet kindness, given though we've never met before

You're the best friend we lonely people have desperately been searching for

You hold our hands through the bad patches

Whoever we are, be it punk, solicitor, rich, young or old

You're an angel in this ruining world

Normal people with problems in everyday situations, can write to you

And your prompt reply will hold the answers

You gracefully accept us for what we are

Everybody looks in their hearts and finds love for you

We all wish we could be like you

Your face so full of so much character

The lines and creases of dedication to helping people interlock with care with your sympathetic eyes

I just love to look at your eyes

Your rough voice sings hand in hand with all the love your lips whisper of

Your complexion holds wonders and secrets of all the
fascinated world
Your womanhood appearance moves with the elegance,
Of the millions of people that write to you
You're a beautiful lady and we all love you
I've only one question to ask you
Where do you go to when you need help?

Darkness Falls

Darkness falls all light is squashed out of sight
No birds sing in contentment, harmony
No flowers swing in the playful wind
Bare surfaces fight the eroding wind
Yelling out silent screams, forever it seems
Ruffled water trickles down bare cracked splitting rock surfaces
The ground looks lifeless
Its twirling granules of rock chase the wind in mock
No squirrels run among the towering stilt like trees
No bushes sing and swing with the bees
No, not even a night watching owl
No ragged wolves to the moon do spookily constantly howl
No man's body brushes alongside nature
Silence attacks with shyness, the ghosts of man
They too will erode into the wind
Being blown away by their untruthful friend, land
No more sun rays, ride with hatred the earth
Darkness works all year round, the Earth has been crushed
Happiness cries with the mist
Rolling around like balls, the past mixes with the rest of time
Everything is now the same, it's a human's lowest crime
Darkness falls with the water fountains

Together they rejoice the departure of all humankind
Only the scarce stilt like trees mix with the darkness
No breathing animals trade innocence for the greediness of
the sufferers
Darkness fans and silence hums its favourite tunes
It's peaceful now, there's no humans
No cars, no lorries, no roads, no houses
Only the wind and the darkness
The day is powerless.

But Still, I Don't Feel Any Different

But still, I don't feel any different
Even looking at the glistening sun
It makes me listen but I still feel numb
I walk through the yellow tipped heads of daffodils
I feel the pleasure but still it's not pleasant
Ignorant people make me laugh
But still, I don't feel any different
Over the seas I travel, crying in my craft
The tears that spill do my feelings kill
Through the evolution of time. Happiness I seek
Love will never find the meek
Seasons circle around and around
Gathering up time, as though it were a wasteful crime
But still, I don't feel any different
True love is only way
But the love in my heart shall stay
People disturb innocently the sadness in my weeping soul
Oh God will they ever know how I moan
How I cry like an overgrown melting man made of snow
Moving around like an impetuous groan
I search for a new hope
Why with life I really must reason

But still, I don't feel any different
Oh, why oh God, did I fall in love
This agonising pain makes life so unpleasant
Now over my heart I wear a protective glove
For you, you'll never invade my infected heart again
Life is so important
To love is a succeeding joyous gain
But still, I don't feel any different
Dreaming is all I can do
Hoping with them that I'll be allowed to love you
In years from now I'll cry a tear, a lonely tear
Year after year and still I'll cry
But still I don't feel any different.

Nothing I Can Do

Nothing I can do
Nothing I can say on the way outta here
No reason to stay
Too long I've been the fool
Too long in the river of despair
Alone in this world of ridicule
On the way to heaven, I climb the stairs
Pain has become my only pleasure
The blood that dries is my only treasure
The razor blade my constant bedfellow
You mock the pain that's made me hollow
Nothing I can do
Nothing I can say
On the way outta here
No reason to stay
The glass that surrounds me
I cannot reach out to you
No matter how hard I plea
Her cries, they suffocate me
Too long I've been the fool
Too long in the river of despair
More in this world of ridicule
On the way to heaven,

I climb the stairs I've played my part
I've been the reluctant hero
I've taken the punches
Received the blows
Still praying for a miracle
I know it's time to go.

My Darling Protecting Angel

Today seems so much shorter than yesterday
The clouds float higher
They the veils, the winds, do sow
Sprinkling spray, which flows free and long
Then any truth the world does know
Rivers of freedom for you and me
You my darling, the advance of time can never be delayed
long enough
For our hands to caress, to stroke each other's hearts with
warmth
You inspire my soul to new momentous heights
Soaring higher than the clouds that ride the skies
My tears no longer swim with continuous flowing rivers
You have brought a new and encouraging hope to my world
A love so tender, so deserving of praise
For these gifts I love you, admire and adore you.

Sarah

Sarah, giver of sensuous kisses
Beholder of great unseen beauty
I love you most dearly
More than the stars that shine above
Alone in the moonlight
More with great strength
Than the winds strive to wipe out the forgotten heroes of the
scarlet night
I love you
Forever the words glide from my tongue
They dance, gaily singing, of my newly found sun,
Sarah.

A Ghost Alone

Standing surrounded by people
The world revolving, converging
Running by unseeing
Not hearing my whisper, my cries
Except me, remove me from this darkness
Pull me by my hand
So I am no longer a watcher
Take my hand
So I am no longer a stranger.

Enough of Purgatory

Let me live
Or let me die
Haven't I paid enough for my sins?
Can true forgiveness can I seek
When I don't believe, I deserve it
Am capable of it
What would it be like to be of free spirit
Of lightness held by innocence.

If Life's a Shower of Rain

Life's a shower of rain.

Raining in tears.

As rain comes and goes

So do the tears from our eyes.

Thunder and lightning are the arguments and violence of the unsettled

Arguments of the unsettled marriages.

As like the rain, it is always with us.

As the sun little does shine,

Happiness is little of mine.

Feelings We All Have

Feelings are things we all do know of
Things that can break us down
Of the things that can restore our lives
Feelings of past and present
And of times to come
These feelings of sadness and sorrow
Feelings of loneliness when alone
Feelings of lost feelings
When love is lost
But there are feelings of joy and happiness
Feeling joyful when at peace
Peace with all men
Peaceful with life and all
Feeling sleepy and content, with our dreams of us dreamers
Feeling contentment of the good we all can do.

What Am I to Do

What am I to do?
Feelings going through me,
Feelings I can't control.
These feelings I loathe.
Hate, hate, hate
That's all the world is for.
What's the point in living?
Through this day and age of war.

Exam

Sitting in an exam
Sitting next to you is Sam
He's just shaking
And you're just wishing, you weren't there in that exam
Your stomach's flying and you feel like you're dying
And now little Di is crying.

Feeling All Alone

When you're feeling all alone, feeling depressed and sad
Because no one's taking any notice of you,
Your feelings or ways within you
You just wonder what the point is,
Of living in hate and sorrow, of loneliness of departure
Why do people hate you, what's wrong with you?
You ask yourself time and time again, after love has gone past
your window
Winter never leaves your soul, it's within you for all time.

A Half-Made Doll

A half-made doll is all that is done.
A body with no clothing,
A head with no hair.
That's all that is done,
Of a half-made doll.
The maker is not dumb,
Only she dislikes the art of making dolls.
The maker is not lazy,
For all are different in skills.
For all are different in likes and dislikes.

Christmas

As I walk through the streets, I can hear the carol singers.
The stars are twinkling in the sky, as they hear the people laughing.
Oh, what joy Christmas brings for all
Rich or poor, young or old.
There is joy for all.
Blazing log fires,
Shadows dancing on the walls.
The goose browns in the oven,
As the mince pies are mixed.
The old man is selling hot chestnuts from his old pushcart.
There are presents around the tree.
And under the pictures there is mistletoe,
Where the young ones kiss, and the old remember.

The Way That We Live

I know very little of the world
That we live in
But I know enough about the way that we live.
The way we live in sin and darkness,
We little do we care
Of the homeless and sick.
But do care for the rich.
I know enough to hate mankind,
That hates love and peace.
But likes destroying it.
I am one in a million.
Who hates the way that we live in.
But little can I do,
Because of the number that lives this way.
We've half destroyed the place that we live
We so little do care of the way that we live.

Dream

When you can't see no point in living
Just close your eyes and dream
Dream, and just dream
For no one will mind
For we all need to dream
To dream all our troubles away.

It's All So Silly

It's all so silly the things we do
the great big world and all its fools
God in so many words did say
peace will come through my name
all that came are wars stating
who's to own the holy land
this alone seems pointless
it's useless
these religious groups are making wars out of the good word
pointless greed
taking all the food we need
fighting over money that makes us so alone
why, why, why
it's all so silly
it don't need be
it can be changed for you and me.

A Fly

A fly does fly above my head
Circling around and around
He flies up and down.
What he thinks I do not know
For a creature he is all of his own.
He flies alone, high and low.
He views his sights from his poor eyesight.
His wings are crisp, as are his silent whispers.
No one hears him, nor understands him.
For he flies alone, high and low, above my head.
As silent as the grass in spring time.

People Laughing with Joy

People laughing with happiness
Morning birds singing with joy
Morning birds singing with happiness
These pleasant sounds come to my ears,
To make me feel better,
Not than for worse
The not quite silent messages of the unseen
God into our souls does come
The wind blows through the gentle swaying tree tops
That we little hear and little see
Rainwater glides down the sloping cliff
Making a river for all the fish
The soft crispin' noise under my feet, made from the icicles
of dew
Of the early morning spring.

You Didn't Really
Kill Yourself

If nothing seems to be going right.
Then just do yourself in, in the middle of the night
No one will mind, if you've got a mind.
For no one cares if you're dead.
Because of your wear and tear,
You didn't really kill yourself.
The world outside did kill yourself.
And many others just like yourself.

Hut 5

I am a hut
Not a very big hut
But a lot of people can get inside of me,
When it need be
I'm grey outside with dirt on me.
From the wind
But inside I'm nice and clean
I have desks and chairs for people to sit at
And a big blackboard to be written upon
I am quite new, not old am I
My name and number are Hut 5.

I Am What I Am

I am what I am
I can't change by dressing to fashion
And trying to act like a dragon
All fierce and unkind, in the inside all round
Shouting and swearing,
It can't change anything
People destroy others by nosing into their lives
Telling them what to wear and to swear
Can we live the way we are?
Do we have to keep saying,
I am what I am?

I Haven't Yet Told You

Miss please don't go, please I need you
Please miss don't go
I need the tender loving from your heart
I need the tender touch of your hand
Please miss, please don't go
Why didn't you tell me of your leaving?
When I haven't even told you,
Of the true love I only hold for you
I couldn't stand a single day
Knowing you weren't there
To give your tender loving,
From the centre of your heart
No one told me of your leaving
Because no one cares of my feelings
For you're the only person,
My love will ever be going to.

True Love

True love is shining from your eyes
True love I've never seen before
True love shining through to my heart
True love I shall hold forever
Never before have I been given such love
You're the first to care, for the one of me
My heart rejoices to see the love shining from your eyes
To the centre of my heart.

The Flower Full of Wonder and Hope

The flower full of wonder and hope will never die
Its petals filled with beauty will never cease of eternal life
In summer months it will flourish, in the warmth of the sun
And in winter will fold away,
Keeping within itself, the warmth of the sun
Sprouting to life once more
When the sun appears, it brings happiness to its children,
With an everlasting smile.

Ghost

Ghost, ghost, there's a ghost
Where? Where? Right there by the chair
I can't see him
I know why, the ghost's a she
That's why I still can't see him
Where? Where? Where is she?
Do you believe in ghosts?
No, I don't believe in ghosts
That's why then
If you did believe in ghosts like me
Then you could see them
Oh no, where has she gone?

A Friend of Death

No longer afraid of death
But death my pathway to a more peaceful way of life
Life here no more my friend
Nowhere to turn to,
But to my new friend death
Life has passed the point of love
No one no longer loves a friend of death.

My Life Seems So Unreal

My sadness, too sad to be true
Days fade into nights of dreams
Never to come true
But still the hope lives within me
For reasons I do not know
So depressed my soul
My mind so empty but still so whole
The memories that drive me
I live to remember
The face I long to see lives within me
I know I should be grateful'
For such happy memories
But how can I be happy, she's no longer with me.

The Look in Their Eyes

The look in their eyes is frightening, bewildering
Hatred glares out, no trust
Only disgust at what you are
They don't care
Evil thoughts escape everywhere
You can't escape it's everywhere
Not a glimpse of a smile
We're heaped in a pile of sadness
Not enough happiness
Distrust feeds on their minds
They're so unkind
The look in their eyes tells me this.

Clouds of Sadness

There's not a cloud in the sky
But my heart holds clouds of sadness
I walk through the streets
Through crowds that never meet
The people's faces so blank
But their minds
Travelling to different places of time
I live to dream
But my mind with all its troubles cannot keep in time
So unsure am I of me
I can no longer ignore the pain in me
I just keep on living for the sun to return
I yearn for the love to return
To love me.

Trapped in Yesterday

They is no now only the past
And dreams of tomorrow never to come to pass
I live for yesterday and die for tomorrow
My hope feeds on dreams of yesterday
My remaining love fights off sorrow of tomorrow
My hearts so strong but yet so weak
It's survived so long but still it weeps
Will tomorrow that's trapped in yesterday
Push through for a new today.

A Jump of Faith

A jump was needed to escape the clutches of evil dwelling
men
Broken knees and fibula, feet, back and jaw too.
My tongue nearly bitten off to remind me to speak kindly
A fall to earth which should have killed me.
Instead brought God into my soul forever to remind me.
The physical pain twists and turns to rid me of the mental
torture
Now the daughter of Christ,
I'm left with scars to remind me.
A new life begins with healing, an end that was so close.
I did not fall from grace but into the loving arms of the Lord.
Taken by hand and heart by God.
He's chosen to forgive me.
Let God catch you, his arms open wide to embrace you.
Remember his words, don't let men condemn you.
As free as soaring birds so high, their cries are enlightening.
Open your arms,
Christ is here to hear you.

I Hardly Dare to Breathe

I hardly dare to breathe as my fingers brush your cheeks
This is the time I've waited for throughout my working week
Laying in sweet abandon, as daylight crashes in
Turning to hold you close again
With no alarm to ring
It's what I dream of
As I'm working through the day
It's what I always dream of
And it's where I want to stay.

The Human Thee

Can't anyone see I need to be free?
Can't anyone listen?
To the human things I need
It's pointless to pretend I'm different from you
But still, I like to pretend
I'm me
I tell myself I'm a winner
A dreamer in all respects
But yet I've got no medals to hang around my neck
My hopes and dreams form my ambition
To make the world completely free
But still all the petitions
Can't change the human thee.

I Love

I love Miss W Newman, with all my heart, soul and mind
Never will my love for her fade away into the dusk of night
When I awake from a night of sleep
All my thoughts at once think of her
Hoping that one day soon
She'll return to the centre of my heart
Forever I'll love her
Never will my love for her depart.

A Language of Poetry

It's so depressing the things I write.
I often wonder if they're right.
People tell me I have a language of poetry.
But who can say if not me?
I would like to write some amusing poetry.
But sadly, alas this is not in me.
My friends can't believe I'm serious
They say I'm a clowner
But do they see the real me? I don't see a pretender.
I see an image fighting for reality
That's not to be found in me.

Dreams Form Hope

There is no now only the past
And dreams of tomorrow never to come
I live for yesterday and die for tomorrow
My hope feeds on dreams of yesterday
My remaining love fights off sorrow of tomorrow
My heart's so strong but yet so weak
It's survived so long
But still, it weeps
Will tomorrow that's trapped in yesterday
Push through for a new today?

I Need to Live to Remember

I need to live to remember
But the sadness has worn me down
And it won't be long before I'm no longer around
But I am still hanging onto my memories of the past
I don't want to die
And my past can't say goodbye
So, I'll live to remember
And hope that time will restart.

For Her Return Is What I Want

Still I'm waiting for miss.
When she'll return I do not know.
I look out of the window.
And wonder where she is.
Does she think of me?
I wonder if she does.
I cry when I remember.
The day she left last summer.
Her laughter and smiles of yesterday.
Keeps me hoping one more day.
Nothing else seems important.
For her return is what I want.

Trying to Forgive

When you're trying to forgive a thing such as this
You try hard not to give it a miss
But your mind echoes on
The misfortunes such as these
For they haunt your being
Your endless nights of crying out in anger and misthoughts
You've been taught to forgive
But forgive you cannot, not these deeds
That have been passed down to you to forgive
As the lord forgives
But forgive you cannot
For these are the deeds of the unforgiving
But there is a light coming from above
A light of the forgiving
That helps us all to forgive of the unforgiving.

In a Cloak of Overtime

I'm a picture that people see
But do not believe
My ambitions and emotions
Wrap my mind in a cloak of overtime
I live in yesterday of ageing time
I need no tomorrow for it's done it's time
Smiles and laughter I borrow
And give them back in a dreamer's ageing sorrow
I am depressing
But I see no good things
Tonight I'll dream and tomorrow too
Hours more of overtime.

To Keep on Living

I've got to keep on living one more day.
Hoping that maybe I'll see her along the way.
And if new love should step into my path.
I'll wonder and I'll ask myself.
Have I got the strength to laugh?
I tell myself I must forget all this pain.
And push my way out of all this rain.
The hours close in and my memories awaken.
Bringing new teardrops that only her voice can stop.
I know I have a choice but who can say why.
I want to keep on living.
So I can no longer cry.

I Need the Music

I know I need the music
That the human mind demands
The songs and melodies their beauty elopes with an everlasting charm
But too it's true that I need the music
That a dreamer can only find
Into the busy streets below
I wonder in and find an enchanting melody
That's in every place of time
All you have to do is listen
And this I'm sure you'll find.

Watching a Scene

Watching a scene on the TV
My body awakens with a chill
My soul knows with a glowing glow
That the words they speak sleep within my cheek
Legends of long ago their meanings I seek
Nations from other worlds
Meeting one another with a meeting love
With a smiling laughter
Truth and justice cut into me like ice
Their meanings longing for a soul
Watching the seasons, I know what they mean
My shimmering body informs me.

Looking at the Moon

Looking at the moon
I wonder how long I'll wait for you.
Will it be soon?
Will I come through?
Before again when I see you.
Clouds cover the shining face of the moon
But still the grins come through
And I won't give up on you
My sadness could steal the good times back
I'll always be wishing you were here to love me
Holding me close never to return back
Never to go leaving me astray
Try to smile, it's the only way
You can survive in a lonely passport world of goodbyes
We're only human but who can say why
We're always saying goodbye.

I Want to Get a One

I want to get a one
In English this is my sun
I work with all force of effort
And to achieve this a hard fight will be fought
My mind explodes with images of practical exercises
Illusions of beautiful poetry in my mind is a security
Of writing to my full
Though my home life is so dull
Writing, writing with an unceasing love
I want to get a one
And all my soul is working
Dreams of painting books with words of beauty
Of villains and crooks
And people in solitary
I want to get a one
This among other things is my sun
Concentrating harshly with stubborn emotions
That are so unwilling to be loved
I want to get a one
In the frightening force of an oncoming exam
My mind of feelings is so crammed
I want to get a one.

The Clowning Clown

Clowning, clowning, clowning clown
Clowns in the circus, clowns in the town
Children laughing, children smiling
Clapping, clapping
Cheering fans gather round
The clowning clown
No more tears, no more fear
Happiness fills the air
To fill our ears because the clowning clown cares
Oops! Bang! He's down on the ground
Laughter he hears, soothes his tears
Smiling, smiling clowning clown
Stay bring happiness
To our circus our town.

Doggies

Doggies, doggies, barking woof
Walking they make a path unclean to tread
So, if you're stepping behind them watch out where you tread
Their teeth drip with saliva when they see a cat
When too you eat, next to you they'll be sat
Sit, stay they'll wait for you like clay
Wagging tails their only way to smile
Pricking ears
Smiling through tears
Many people do fear doggies.

Going Down a One-Way Street

Going down a one way street
No turns no turning back
Loving only dreams
Dreaming of finding love in a one way street
Falling in love time after time
With people who are always turning away from me
Their love never to be mine
They laugh with foolish smiles
Travelling down the road miles and miles
Mocking at my love
They hit out at my kindness
But still I roam down the road
Smiling, I try to overtake the cruelness
With my back so bent it's a danger sign
Like an electric circuit it's on overload
But still they give nothing back.

I Feel Nothing

I feel nothing, my heart is empty
I shall not murder
I shall not squalor
For I shall not die by the curse of the devil I'm so sad my eyes
do cry
When I'm listening to God I know what the future will bring
Miss will return and I'll be rejoicing again
I love her, forever needing her
I shall always await
I shall not give up
Forever and again for her love I'll be waiting.

Where the Wind Blows

When the wind blows, I shall go
Where the winds seize to be
I shall find me
Where I meet my true love
I shall greet
Where are you going?
Why are you going?
To find the real me
Where the wind blows
I shall go
Where the winds cease to be, there my home shall be
To find the real me in a land of make believe
I shall never leave
Where the wind blows l shall go
Where the winds seize to be I shall find me.

Harper, Harper, Baggy Draws

Harper, Harper, baggy draws.
Screams down the corridors.
And wipes the flippen blackboards.
Bald on top, screeching voice.
You look like a soppy wolfhound.
That's why your skin flops down to the ground
You are a moany old faggot
With your face like a faggot
Your trousers are not in the latest fashion
But you're surely louder than any dragon
But still you're a dear old soul
Don't you hit us, don't you dare
Your concord voice is not the flare
Baggy draws, you don't make the laws
Harper, Harper, baggy draws.

Me

As I relax onto a bench on an October's mid-evening night
I try to explain inquiringly that I'm a sorrowful sight
Now here I am only a human I be
But yet I am a ghost no finding a human within me
Do I look strange sat out here in the night?
Will this poem make enough sense to read to thee this night?
Oh God I'm so weary, no love makes sense to me
I'm confused at what I might be
Right or wrong is thee
My hair in my eyes, my heart in my feet
Doth this be me.

Outside Lays John

Outside lays a ditch, in it lays a man
In his wallet lays nothing
For he is not a rich man
Outside his mind lays nothing
In his heart there is a sad song outside there's a bold country
There's a place where his young love will always belong
Around his neck is a rope
You see he couldn't cope
He died a broken man
In heaven his heart is now amend
Like his hanging from a tree
His mind can now be free
Outside lays a ditch, in it lays a man
His body is now only a corpse
Over the earth covered body is set a tombstone
Engraved in the stone are words written alone
Farewell to John.

We Don't Exist

To begin with, neither of us exist
To point out we will never die
Memories are too long and forever lasting
Be truthful always
Don't say what you feel, think of others
Love the continuity
Remind them of their hate
It doesn't give pain, it's just a way of explaining
Walk behind understanding
Prove you're sorry
Don't cuddle, don't begin to smile
You're be loved
And proven trustworthy in time.

In My Twenty-Four Hours

I see two days and a night come and go in my 24 hours
But in your 24 hours you only see a day and a little of the
night
Some people love the sea while others love the land
Or like to be as free as a bird
Flying, admiring the exquisite birds in the high disappearing
sky
Seeing the day fade into a silent carnival blanket of shadows
Seeing the unlit fairground turn into an explosion of light
Turns my magical soul into electricity of dancing imagination
The power of curled cobblestones in the forests of the human
deserted cities
Flashes hums into my wandering mind
In my 24 hours, I experience all time.

Friends Love You Best

Try to keep my puzzling mind together
Remembering the good things people have said
Look back at only the happy memories of yesterday
Always forgive other people's mistakes
But always your own first
Like an arrow to its bow, your faults must be accepted
For your soul to keep it's glow
Move from town to town if you must
You can always return home
Make friends and keep them
No need to get heavy, friends love you best.

Bloody Twits

Bloody twits nicking stuff
No one will listen if you've made a mistake
Learning all the time
Tick-tocking, listen to the chime
Being a true dyke, you don't have to have a bike
Angry, angry no use crying
Don't lie down and beg, you've still got legs
Smile, be true to yourself
Like the winter and summer
Different times, different times
No use being grumpy
Be yourself, but only to yourself
You always have a choice
But you may have to pay the price
Government's promises, government's talking
Not to you or me
Not to the lower classes
No end, no beginning, nor an in between
Just you and me
Just bloody twits.

Parted from Friends

While I'm relentlessly away from my caring friends
The days grow ever longer
The night becomes a scene of tossing bodies
Holding our heavy heads in our hands
Thinking of the day when we parted with family and friends
They come from far away to make me smile
You can't stay too long
The rules and regulations they say not
So cruel they seem
When we'll first meet again on the outside world
Our thoughts will be forever tinged
Then our eyes will cry silent tears in streams
We must only take one day at a time
Our memories winding through our minds
Becoming our lifeline of silent chimes of time
One day we're all be together
But until that day that seems so far away
Think of me as I think of you
All my family and friends we'll be together soon.

Crying Alone

Silent tears, crying alone
Don't let anyone hear
Alone in a square room
I know she'll be cruel
Don't think I can go on
Sweep my life away like a hand to a broom
Shut my eyes tightly so I can't see the con
Silent trees, silent winds
Take away my wings
Should dry away my tears
Give some clay to my heart so it can't get torn apart.

Everybody Needs Somebody

No matter just who you are
Young or old, calm or bold
There's somebody reaching out for you to hold
Waiting for the first time, seems to take forever
Until unexpectedly, a sweetness taps you on your shoulder
Whispers gently for you to come with me
The old timer becomes your caressing teacher
You can now believe true love can be
To be together when the new dawn breaks free
Warm heated bodies sweetly
There's only the first time
So we savour the beauty as we would a rare honeybee
Thank you sweet lady, who held me tenderly
For caressing my body, softly
Chasing my childhood away
Waving goodbye to all the games of ring a roses
Thank you sweet lady,
For greeting me to the new way of breaking free
On how to look on yesterday as only memories
For starting me on the road to knowing the real me
Thank you, oh you sweet lady.

To So Many Friends

To so many friends who mean so much
A simple thank you could never be enough
You've stood by me, never turned away
Accepted me for who I am
God I'm thankful for being gay
For having you as friends
Helping me to see the new light of day
Our own special friendships
Living our lives in a beautiful way
To all my friends all that there is left to say
It's a big thank you to so many friends.

All Day Long I Think of You

All day long I think of you, throughout the night until the new
day's dew
Await my return I do beg of you
Comfort me with kisses in the home we once knew
Your smiles, your sweet eyes I left without thought
This apart from anything is my one and only crime
The pain does grow forever deeper
Sweet darling of time, please say you'll be mine
My arms will keep aching
At the thought of holding you
Until that day we're together once more
Throughout the day, the night
Forever for all time
But until that day, I can only think of you.

To Friends of Human Spirit

To friends of human spirit, so far away
I'll think of you throughout the coming days
Our dreams are of the same merit
Hoping our futures will soon be clear of pain
Of sorrow, of departing
To be like the birds freely flying
Holding green grass
As in the wind it sways in
Laughing at the insane, this becoming our life line
Smiling to repair deepening scars
We watch for each other through the blackening lies
That mould our lives
The day will come when we're together again
My friends of human spirit.

My Friend Guilt

Through the sleet and rain we walk hand in hand
Me and my friend guilt
Guilt too heavy a burden for one to bare
Still it's not a feeling to be shared
So alone I walk through the stormy streets of guilt
Too ashamed to show my face amongst caring friends
High brick walls invisible they remain
So I sit alone, trying endlessly to make amends
Nights become my refuge for nightmares blacked in shame
Help me to feel worthy of someone's love
Cut the chains that bind me to the endless reminder of my one
mistake
Show a little kindness, to help me live
So my love to you I may one day give
Help me through my weakness
So that I may try to remain sane
Through the sleet and rain my sagging soul cries out in vain
Tell me honestly all is forgiven
That a friend to guilt
I no longer have to remain.

My Friends

Please do not feel anxious at what I have to say
But my friends I love you
In the purest, kindest way
For all of you have shown great kindness
In a world so full of hate
Throughout the hard times you've been my friend
For you have shown understanding, not hate
Excepted me, not disowned me, forgiven me
So to you my friends, I raise my glass, thank you.

Meet Me Halfway

Meet me halfway
And I'll show you the way to a friendship filled with happiness
Leave the ignorance of onlookers to yesterday
Give us a chance
Together we'll find a way
I know you're unsure of what the world has in hold for you
So until time indicates your soul to be sure,
With unpressing patience, I'll wait for you
We both agree honesty is the best policy
So reach out for my hand and hold on tight
We'll see it through the night
The sun does rise with a new gleaming light
Happiness can push through to make things right
Live for today
Meet me halfway.

Love Me for I Am Only I

Love me for I am only I
Beneath the sheets that cover us
Like the clouds in a blue sky
Our arms entwine forgiving us of our trespass
Like the birds that sing sweetly
And the crocodiles swim with slyness and ease
Eyes that see and kisses linger
Tongues that taste with the perfume of our mother's womb
Comforting each other
A friend and judge
Our bodies explore each other of our inadequate intentions
Tensions fly and knock us over like the wings of a butterfly
Love me, for I am only I.

Goodbye Miss

Goodbye miss, for years you ruled my life
Farewell to you I must say
Now my days are my own
You locked away my future in your hands
You stole my heart and replaced it with a sadness too true I've
finally gotten over you
I can now start again and replace those years with a new joy
While you were here
When my days were filled only with anguish and fear
You gave me hope
So I must thank you miss
For you pointed out the way to true happiness
To being a true woman
A woman who loves only women
So this I can now say to you without feeling blue,
Goodbye miss.

Loneliness

Loneliness sucks into my disappearing smile
No longer allowed to smile wishfully at a wandering beauty
A sweet lady who smiles teasingly
Though not at me, just another face
Unsure if the object be male or a hopeful lesbian
Memories of unsure, golden days
Scratch at the hopeful souls that no longer choose to be free
Loneliness, the undignified disease
Pacts of sollom filled people hunt for the cure,
Love
Doctors from near and far,
Hide the humans fear with fancy named bottles that have no
reproach
Forgetting the unchangeable fact that a tear must fall
Our minds fade into darkness, immobilised by fear
No longer willing to be loving, only increasing loneliness.

Ask Me No Questions

Ask me no questions and I'll tell you no lies
Hold my hand and I'll stay by your side
Kiss me quickly and I'll stay by your side
Kiss me quickly, kiss me slow
Hold me tightly, never let go
Look into my eyes, what do you see
Love so pure just for you and me
So ask no questions and I'll stay by your side.

Lost Again

Lost again
Looking through the dismal rain of defeats
Will my time come to stand and share in the glory of being a
winner?
Will people stand and applaud me as I sweat and strive for
peace
Walk a few yards and darkness can entwine itself around me
Forever lost, a looser
Pull me up from this world wind of despair
Unchain my sadness so your happiness I may share
Show me the road that leads to the cotton fields of
contentment
Show me a rainbow where my heart can rise and dance to the
music of being free
Of the world allowing me to be free.

Don't Twist Me

Don't say you love me while doing the things you do.
You're hurting me, not loving me.
Making me your favourite.
All I wanna do is play cops and robbers, to be with my friends
Stop playing with me.
You're disfiguring my mind, my future.
Don't put your hands there, that's not for you to do.
That's mine and mine alone.
Why does your mind work the way it does?
You're cruel to make me love you.
I want to be a child, not twisted by you.

Coming Together

Frustrations crying out for the tender touch
Whispering gently to the giver of sensuous kisses
For that my cold soul may cry out in joy
Coming further to the end of tunnel of love
Coming slowly closer, to the peak of enjoyment
Help me, help me
To reach the pot of gold that lies waiting at the beginning of every rainbow
At the end of tonight when finally you and I come to the beginning,
Of the coming together, so right
In the strong winds of this world you may sit upon my shoulders
I may bend and sway but I will always hold you up.

A Day with You

A day with you and I smile delightfully for the first time in years
A week with you and my forgotten dreams begin to come true
A month with you and my heart begins to dance to the sweet melody of refreshing love, young and pure
My darling lover, my friend so true
Oh how much, my soul does love you
Just six months with you and my whole life upturns to the motion of your body
Just nine months with you
And my timeless journey into paradise begins with a single laugh your tenderness gives
My darling love, my friend so dear
When I'm beside you I never fear
A year with you and I am so happy
To be with you for a day is too short
A year with you and my life has
Only just begun.

The absence of sound deafens
The brutality of the wind sharpens
The absence of humans gladdens

The Waiting Room

We don't mind sitting in the waiting room
For the good doctors that we see
They don't look at their computer screens
They look at the real you and me
The receptionist's all busy with phone calls and paperwork
behind the scenes
How they don't lose their patience is always beyond me.
The nurses are gentle and kind to the likes of you and me
Physical or emotional and mental health too
They listen when we're breaking and help us off our knees.
When time is running over
Remember these are the best in town
They go beyond the call of duty
To help you and me.

Ingram Content Group UK Ltd.
Milton Keynes UK
UKHW020626160323
418667UK00014B/1236